TOOLS FOR CAREGIVERS

- **F&P LEVEL:** C
- **WORD COUNT:** 32
- **CURRICULUM CONNECTIONS:** nature, farming

Skills to Teach

- **HIGH-FREQUENCY WORDS:** the, they, we
- **CONTENT WORDS:** corn, ears, eat, grow, husks, kernels, leaves, off, pick, plant, pull, shoots, stalks, tall, yum
- **PUNCTUATION:** exclamation points, periods
- **WORD STUDY:** /k/, spelled c (corn); long /e/, spelled ea (ears, eat, leaves); long /o/, spelled ow (grow); /oo/, spelled oo (shoots)
- **TEXT TYPE:** information report

Before Reading Activities

- Read the title and give a simple statement of the main idea.
- Have students "walk" through the book and talk about what they see in the pictures.
- Introduce new vocabulary by having students predict the first letter and locate the word in the text.
- Discuss any unfamiliar concepts that are in the text.

After Reading Activities

Explain to readers that farmers plant corn. They plant the kernels in rows. Look at more pictures of corn growing in fields. Have readers ever seen corn or other crops going in a field? What do the stalks and ears look like? Have readers draw their own stalks and ears of corn growing in a field.

Tadpole Books are published by Jump!, 5357 Penn Avenue South, Minneapolis, MN 55419, www.jumplibrary.com

Copyright ©2023 Jump. International copyright reserved in all countries. No part of this book may be reproduced in any form without written permission from the publisher.

Editor: Jenna Gleisner **Designer:** Molly Ballanger

Photo Credits: narvikk/iStock, cover (left); Anastasiia Skorobogatova/Shutterstock, cover (right); AlenKadr/Shutterstock, 1; Denys Prokofyev/Dreamstime, 2ml, 3; Stevanovicigor/Dreamstime, 2bl, 4–5; Andrey Krupenko/Shutterstock, 2mr, 2br, 6–7; Andersen Ross Photography Inc/Getty, 8–9; Alexey Stoip/Shutterstock, 2tl, 10–11; Jamie Grill/Getty, 2tr, 12–13; BLOOMimage/Getty, 14–15; Artikom jumpamoon/Shutterstock, 16.

Library of Congress Cataloging-in-Publication Data
Names: Sterling, Charlie W., author.
Title: Corn / by Charlie W. Sterling.
Description: Minneapolis, MN: Jump!, Inc., (2023)
Series: See a plant grow! | Includes index. | Audience: Ages 3–6
Identifiers: LCCN 2021047465 (print) | LCCN 2021047466 (ebook)
ISBN 9781636906966 (hardcover)
ISBN 9781636906973 (paperback)
ISBN 9781636906980 (ebook)
Subjects: LCSH: Corn—Life cycles—Juvenile literature.
Classification: LCC SB191.M2 S6295 2023 (print) | LCC SB191.M2 (ebook) | DDC 633.1/5—dc23/eng/20211001
LC record available at https://lccn.loc.gov/2021047465
LC ebook record available at https://lccn.loc.gov/2021047466

SEE A PLANT GROW!

CORN

by Charlie W. Sterling

TABLE OF CONTENTS

Words to Know 2

Corn 3

Let's Review! 16

Index 16

WORDS TO KNOW

ears

husks

kernels

leaves

shoots

stalks

CORN

kernel

We plant kernels.

They grow shoots.

stalk

They grow stalks.

leaf

They grow leaves.

They grow tall!

They grow ears.

We pick the ears.

husk

We pull off the husks.

We eat corn.

Yum!

LET'S REVIEW!

Corn plants have many parts. What part is circled below?

INDEX

ears 11, 12
husks 13
kernels 3
leaves 7

pick 12
plant 3
shoots 5
stalks 6